ROME

THE FASCINATION OF ART AND HISTORY

1

Giancarlo Gasponi

ROME
THE FASCINATION OF ART AND HISTORY

Artistic collaboration
Rouhyeh Avaregan

Text
Glauco Cartocci

Picture comments
Glauco Cartocci e Giancarlo Gasponi

 Euroedit · Trento

Not eternity, but close to it

A history so complex that at times it seems to bear clear traces of some superior design; and yet so disorderly as to appear to our eyes to have almost always been the product of blind chance and paradox.

Almost three thousand years lived in a monumental dimension; in a kind of distorting lens that confuses and superposes heroic and shabby gestures, absolute values and miserable facts, grandeur and stupidity, all reduced to one and the same scale.

The assumption that the city's vicissitudes were intimately interwoven with the destiny of the world was both a profound conviction and a feeling of inevitableness, a source of strength and pride and a kind of convict's chain. Almost three thousand years. That's not eternity, but they can be too many. For anybody. Rome included.

The birth of the city, 753 B.C., is a conventional date, established by Varro on the basis of tradition. But the period is considered credible even by archeologists, and the city's original nucleus must have been situated between the Palatine and the Quirinal. The original Forum is to be found in the valley between the two hills, a place of meeting and the site of markets.

The first 250 years, the epoch of the seven Kings, constitute a phase of definition of the military and political structure. During the reign of the last three monarchs Rome was under the dominion of the Etruscans, though this did not lack positive aspects, especially from the cultural point of view.

The city developed on the five hills next to the two on which it had been founded. The Cloaca Maxima was built and the area of the Forum was drained and fully reclaimed.

In 509 B.C. the city entered its republican period, which was to see the birth of the democratic system based on the continuous search for an equilibrium between the will of the Senate and that of the people. The Romans showed themselves to possess considerable capacities in coming to grips with practical problems of every kind: canals to convey drinking water and liquid wastes, walls, military structures, camps for their legions. The early centuries of the city's history saw construction activities prevail over the figurative arts, considered devoid of utility. But towards the end of the Republic, esthetic values assimilated following the conquest of Greece found a place in Rome's cultural patrimony and the considerable techniques that had been developed began to be used for beautifying the city; it was at this time that mere building gave way to architecture.

In 390 B.C. the Gauls invaded Rome from the North. Brennus, Rome's first great adversary, set the city on fire and threatened it with slavery, eventually to be defeated by Furius Camillus. Construction of the colossal defences, later to be known as the "Servian walls", was commenced in this period and continued for a century and a half. Their perimeter reached about 11 kilometres and contained 15 gates. Rome extended her influence in a succession of wars and by the year 265 B.C. she had achieved practically complete hegemony over the peninsula. The clash with Carthage, a strong sea power, became inevitable. More than a century of wars (264-146 B.C.) saw Rome get the better of her great rival, and this meant dominion over the entire Mediterranean basin.

The next century was characterized by considerable outward expansion and important social and political ferments at home. Rome reached Asia and Gaul, subjected Numidia, and threw back the barbarian invasions from the North. At the same time there developed grave conflicts between the classes that existed within the Republican system: they culminated in the rivalry between the senatorial faction led by Sulla and the popular faction, of which Marius was the leading spirit. And that meant civil war.

The first triumvirate – government by the generals Crassus and Pompey (both of the senatorial party) and Caesar, sustained by the popular classes, dates to 62 B.C.: it constituted an attempt of re-establishing some kind of social equilibrium. Nevertheless, the contrast between Pompey and Caesar could not but explode. The latter prevailed and enjoyed an absolute dominion over Rome from 48 to 44 B.C., year of the conspiracy that was to kill him, recalled by literature as "the Ides of March".

Some important urban works date to the period that goes from Sulla to Caesar, including the two bridges that link Tiberina Island, the first rational layout of the Capitol and buildings like the Tabularium (the state archive), Pompey's Theatre and the portico in the Martian Fields. Caesar reorganized the Roman Forum, where he constructed the Basilica Julia, and opened a forum of his own, adorning it with the temple of Venus Genitrix.

Somewhat later, Octavianus concentrated all the powers in his person. In 27 B.C. the Senate accorded him the honorary title of "Augustus" and sanctioned his absolute "imperium" over the enormous territory dominated by Rome. Augustus made Rome worthy of being "capital of the world": he put marble in the place of wood, reconstructed a large number of public buildings and added many new ones, among them the Temple of Apollo, the enormous porticos, the Theatre of Marcellus, the Ara Pacis, his mausoleum in the Martian Fields. He also opened the Forum Augusti and erected the sumptuous imperial palace on the Palatine Hill.

Henceforth the emperor was to have the possibility also of reorganizing urban areas without having to worry about what was already there. This factor, together with the frequent fires that razed entire quarters to the ground, constituted the beginning of planning on a larger scale and therefore urban design and layout. Indeed, the Augustan age saw the entire problematic of architecture and town planning codified in a single treatise: Vitruvius' De Re Aedificatoria. The forms and types of the Greek tradition were examined and classified, together with the Italic construction experience, be it Etruscan, Tuscan or Roman. It was a complex "theorization" of classical culture that was to constitute an excellent point of reference for both the Renaissance and Neoclassicism.

The four emperors who followed Augustus from 14 to 68 A.D. belonged to the Julio-Claudian dynasty. The last of them, Nero, a controversial figure shrouded in legend, drew up a precise master plan, with regularly laid out quarters and streets: the mysterious fire of 68 A.D. facilitated the operation and constituted yet one more thing for which tradition blames the emperor. But the Domus Aurea, Nero's immense imperial palace, lasted only a few decades.

Vespasian, Titus and Domitian, the Flavians, accentuated the city's development. During their rule the ancient Circus Maximus was restructured, the Colosseum was put up and the Forum of Peace, conceived as an art museum, was opened, as also the Odeon in the Martian Fields and the nearby Stadium of Domitian (today Piazza Navona).

The second century A.D. and the beginning of the third constitute the vertex of the empire's historic parabola: it is not mere chance that those who occupy its highest office in this period are figures rich in wisdom and farsightedness, rather than possessors of mere military virtues.

Trajan built the forum, the baths and the markets that bear his name. Hadrian, just as great as his predecessor, completely forsook military expeditions in favour of spirituality and culture. The grandiose Temple of Venus and Rome, the Villa-City at Tivoli, the complete reconstruction of the Pantheon and the Mausoleum (now Castel Sant'Angelo) with the bridge that leads to it are all due to him.

The epoch of the Antonines and the Severi saw the erection of the Temples of Antoninus and Faustina, the Temple of Hadrian, the columns of Antoninus Pius and Marcus Aurelius; the Septizonium, a grandiose seven-floor structure, the Arch of Septimius Severus, and the Baths of Caracalla, an immense polyfunctional complex.

A critical period commenced in 235 A.D., year of the death of Alexander Severus: if we were to compare the empire to a living organism, we could recognize the profound fatigue and exhaustion deriving from too much burnt energy, the inevitable passage from maturity to old age. Indeed, there now followed half a century of anarchy and continuous successions on the imperial throne (as many as 22 emperors), accompanied by the continuous threat of barbarian invasions. Aurelian surrounded the city with a new ring of walls (19 kilometers) and this resumption of the construction of defensive structures is altogether symptomatic.

In 284 A.D. Diocletian divided the empire into four prefectures, thus sanctioning the end of Rome's centrality and shifting power towards the East. The last great imperial constructions in the city were to be the Diocletian Baths, the Basilica of Maxentius, the Arch of Constantine and the baths on the Quirinal.

But the historical fact of Christianity being accorded freedom of cult (313 A.D.) was the beginning of a new era and for the city it meant being transformed from caput of the world of antiquity into the centre of Christianity.

Right from the beginning, the new cult buildings, baptistries and basilicas, displayed a decided spatial and artistic sensitivity. Three of the patriarchal basilicas date to the Constantinian period: St. Peter in Vatican, St. John in Lateran, and St. Paul Outside the Walls. S. Maria Maggiore, the fourth, also known as Liberiana (after Pope Liberius), dates to about 360. Henceforth, indeed, it fell to popes to be associated with monumental and urban events. In 476 A.D. the Empire of the West formally ceased to exist.

The centuries that followed were dense with events, but town planning and art in the city went through a long period of stasis and rather than being planned, events in this field were casual. In the 7th and 8th century Rome still constituted an exception with respect to the desolate cultural panorama of the rest of the peninsula. Artists from the East worked in S. Maria Antiqua, Sant'Agnese, executing paintings and mosaics. The Byzantine court had settled a substantial Eastern colony in the area of the Forum Boarium, and for this reason Romans referred to it as "ripa graeca"; the products of this period are S. Giorgio al Velabro, S. Maria in Cosmedin and S. Maria in Domnica. Between the end of the 8th and the beginning of the 9th century a new school of mosaic artists formed in Rome and worked in S. Prassede, S. Cecilia and S. Marco. The Carolingian epoch had dawned: the Pope received important land donations from Charlemagne and these began to constitute the embryo of the Church State that was to develop and last right into the nineteenth century.

Following the end of the Carolingian empire, Rome was once again laid open to attack: the Arabs sacked St. Peter's in 846, and immediately afterwards Leo IV constructed the Vatican's defensive system now known as the "Leonine walls". In 932 Hadrian's Tomb became the fortified hub of these defences, the "Castello". This brings us to the 12th and 13th century: Rome remained outside the cultural approach of the communes, which claimed autonomy with respect to the Empire. Romanesque art therefore touched the city only in a very marginal manner: the bell tower of S. Maria in Cosmedin, S. Clemente, the total restructuring of S. Maria in Trastevere. But towards the end of the 13th century we again find important figures. The great Arnolfo da Cambio, marble and mosaic workers like the Cosmati, Iacopo Torriti and Pietro Cavallini.

From 1305 to 1371 the Papacy was transferred to Avignon: for the city this was a period of economic eclipse that was to cause the city to lag far behind other centres of culture. But under Nicholas V (1447-55) Rome once again opened her arms to artists and scholars, among them Leon Battista Alberti and Bernardo Rossellino; for the first time after many years there was again talk about a planned urban layout, a topic that was to be further developed under the pontificates of Paul III and Sixtus IV.

The importance of the Vatican and the area around Ponte, which had gradually grown since the return from Avignon, was sanctioned by the transformation of Castel S. Angelo into a sumptuous residence of the Popes. The fortifications of the ancient monument were enlarged and it was definitively connected to the Vatican palaces by means of the covered passage on top of the Leonine Wall. Bramante was at work in Rome at the beginning of the 16th century and dedicated himself to the Cloister of Peace at S. Pietro in Montorio and, above all, the first project for the new St. Peter's. Indeed, Julius II (1503-13) commissioned him to pull down the ancient Constantinian basilica, and the architect did this with such zeal as to be dubbed the "master wrecker".

The very important pontificate of Paul III Farnese (1534-49) coincided with the beginning of the Counter-Reformation. Michelangelo built the tomb of Julius II in S. Pietro in Vincoli, worked at Palazzo Farnese and in the Pauline Chapel; from 1536 to 1441 he painted the Universal Judgement. In 1547 he was appointed architect of St. Peter's. Via Paola was laid out under the same Pope and a start was also made with Via Trinitatis, which was later to become the principal axis of the "plan" of Sixtus V. Midway through the century Michelangelo worked at S. Giovanni de' Fiorentini, put up Porta Pia, and laid out Piazza del Campidoglio.

Elected in 1585, Sixtus V changed the face of Rome in no more than five years. He completed the cupola of St. Peter's, enlarged the Quirinal, rebuilt the Lateran, laid out the Felice Aqueduct. Moreover, he conceived a large-scale town plan (the so-called "Sixtine system"), which consists of nine rectilinear road axes joining the existing urban "poles".

At the beginning of the 17th century the Basilica of St. Peter was "completed" by Carlo Maderno, who transformed the central scheme into a longitudinal one and created the facade, two operations that caused a great deal of discussion. That was the beginning of the great season of Roman Baroque. The century left a great imprint on the city in the form of some great compositions and a thousand minor ones. The Baroque style is probably more consonant than others with the "nature" of the place, with what has been called Rome's "vital disorder".

A series of grandiose realizations followed under Urban VIII (1623-44): Palazzo Barberini, the Triton and Bee Fountains, the works of Bernini inside St. Peter's; S. Carlino and the Oratorio dei Filippini. The pontificate of Innocent X (1644-55) was marked by the laying out of Piazza Navona (Palazzo Pamphili, Fountain of the Rivers, S. Agnese), the remaking of St. John in Lateran, the works of Pietro da Cortona.

Alexander VII (1655-67) had S. Maria della Pace built by Cortona, S. Ivo by Borromini and S. Andrea and the baldachin in St. Peter's by Bernini. But the grandiose operation that distinguishes his reign is Bernini's laying out of St. Peter's Square with its colonnade, corridors and the Scala Regia. The great cycle commenced with the Renaissance was about to end and – as always – the end was not sudden: Baroque fizzled out in a large number of less striking initiatives that followed already known paths and added nothing new.

The cultural and artistic importance of Rome, as also of Italy as whole, was in clear decline in the 18th century, a reflection of political and economic facts. There were no outstanding figures among the Pontiffs and the architects, the epoch of great events had decidedly come to an end; ground was being gained by initiatives of conservation and collecting works of art, archeological studies, theories of esthetics. Rome was a city "in the fashion", with all the implications of the terms, negative ones not excluded. Among the realizations of the epoch we find Alessandro Specchi's Porto di Ripetta, a valid attempt of exploiting the Tiber as a vital part of the urban landscape, and the facades of S. Giovanni de' Fiorentini and S. Maria Maggiore. But the best known works of the entire century are the Trevi Fountain by N. Salvi and the stairway of Trinità dei Monti by De Sanctis. The former can be considered as still forming part of the Baroque, while the latter is a typical creation of its day and sees monumentality abandoned in favour of a formal and almost decorative grace.

The 19th century opened with Napoleon's domination in Rome (1809 13). The "second city of the French Empire" was made the object of grandiose plans that comprised the rehabilitation of entire quarters, valorization of archeological areas, the laying out of parks. But practically everything remained on paper.
In 1814 Pius VII returned to a city with a strongly declining population, unhealthy hygienic conditions and suffering from the economic crisis. He nevertheless attempted to continue along the road of public works, but (with the exception of Piazza del Popolo) could not achieve a great deal. The end of his reign in 1823 ushered in twenty years of depression that culminated in the cholera epidemic of 1838. The long pontificate of Pius IX (1846-78) was full of political events, but the sole initiative at the urban level was the creation of the quarter around what is today Via Nazionale. 1870 saw Rome annexed by Italy; the "breach" at Porta Pia marked the end of the temporal power of the Popes.

No longer "caput mundi" for many a long century, but – perhaps – once again Capital, Rome now entered the phase that – to our mind – has lasted to this day.
It is true that since then we have crossed the watersheds that separate the Kingdom from the Fascist regime and the Republic; that we have passed through two world wars and social and technological upheavals that are enormous when compared with the length of time in which they occurred. But something remained constant in more than a century and is, unfortunately, an absence: the absence of a city image in step with the times, an "ideal" model (or, more modestly, a not overly vague assumption regarding the city's future development).
The "Third Rome" was never born; it is everything that is neither Ancient Rome nor Papal Rome. For this reason we still feel children of Porta Pia, and for this reason we do not distinguish the Altar of the Fatherland from Via della Conciliazione, from EUR and the work for the Olympic Games in 1960: all this is contemporary history.
The while we wait for better times.

The Fascination of Art and History

5

6 ▷

9

13

14

15 ▷

16

17

19

20▷

29

30

37   38

48

49 ▷

50 ▷▷

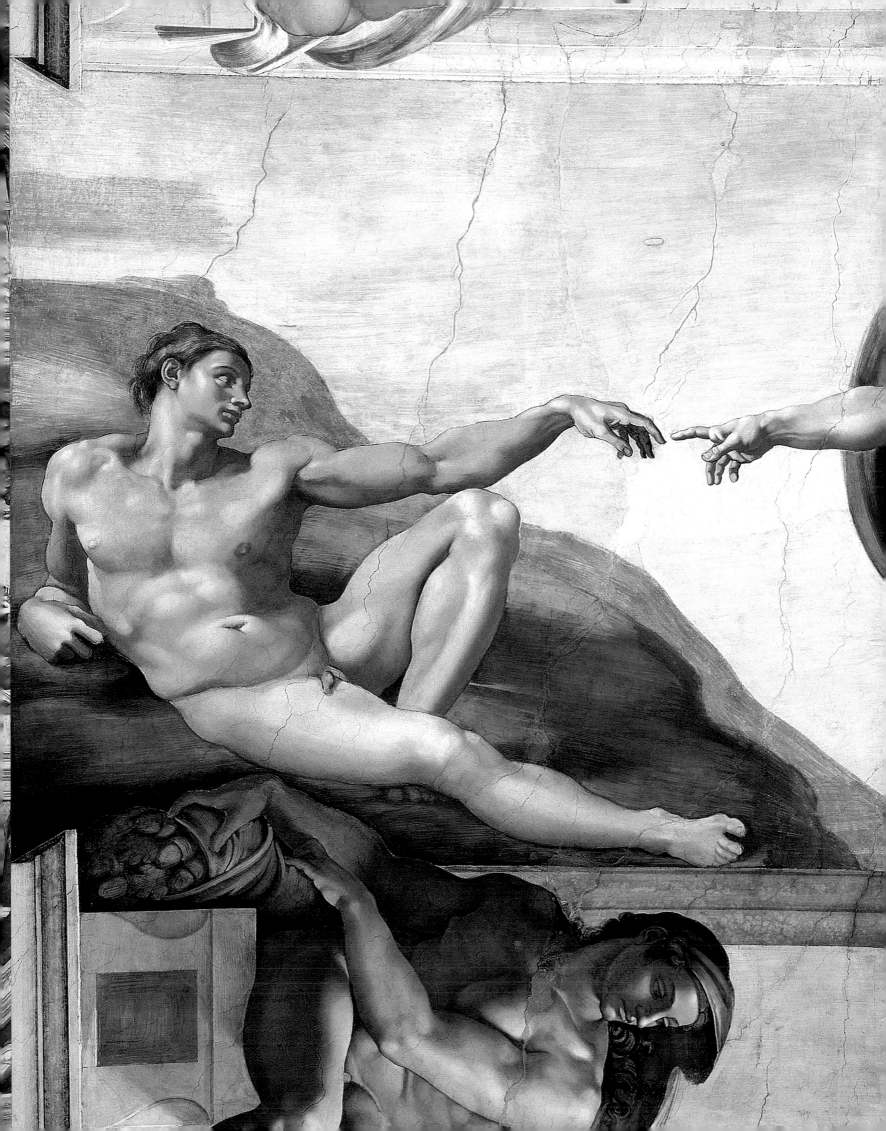

53

54

CLEMENS XII PONT MAX
AQVAM VIRGINEM
COPIA ET SALVBRITATE COMMENDATAM
CVLTV MAGNIFICO ORNAVIT
ANNO DOMINI MDCCXXXV PONTIF VI

PERFECIT   BENEDICTVS XIV   PON MAX

61

69

70

PIVS·IIII·PONT·MAX
PORTAM·IN·HANC·AMPLI
TVDINEM·EXTVLIT
VIAM·FLAMINIAM
STRAVIT·ANNO·III

77

void and full. At the centre of the fine paving pattern, Marcus Aurelius has been an immobile spectator of sackings, ruin, grandeur and decadence.

Palazzo Nuovo houses the Capitoline Museum, the world's first public museum. Its collection of classical sculptures, enriched by numerous Popes, was opened to the public in 1734. Its precious works include many Roman copies of Greek masterpieces. Outstanding is a collection of busts depicting Roman emperors, poets and philosophers (No.23). In Photograph No.24, a window behind Amor and Psyche (3rd/2nd century B.C.) frames the solemn facade of Palazzo Senatorio.

26 - Fragment of the **Statue of Costantine**. Palazzo dei Conservatori – the Conservatori were the supreme magistrates of republican Rome – constitutes the right-hand wing of Michelangelo's harmonious Capitol Square. It was put up by G. Della Porta (c. 1563) on the site of a medieval building resting on the remains of the Tabularium, the state archive of ancient Rome.

Inside it hides a large colonnaded courtyard adorned by many sculptures, including fragments of a statue of Apollo and a colossal one of Constantine. Part marble and part bronze, the latter stood in the Basilica of Maxentius and seems to have been smashed when its vault collapsed.

27 - **Fountain of the Tortoises**. An exquisite masterpiece of elegance and lightness, this is one of the fountains Romans love best and it is also greatly admired by any foreign visitors who manage to find it, seeing that it is well off the principal tourist routes, hidden away in the tiny Mattei Square. It was designed by Giacomo della Porta and executed by Taddeo Landini around 1585. This delicious monument feasts the eye with its extreme grace. Four ephebes, whose movements are not of this earth, sustain four tortoises while they drink from the upper basin… a game, a rite, a dance.

28 - Sunset on the Tiber at the level of **Ponte S.Angelo**, the most beautiful of Rome's ancient bridges, with Hadrian's Tomb and St. Peter's in the background. Built by Hadrian in 136 A.D. to give access to his mausoleum, the bridge later became the sole direct crossing point to reach St. Peter's. In 1668 it was adorned with ten statues of angels designed by Bernini, splendid examples of Roman Baroque (see Photo No.20). Hadrian's Tomb has pulsated in unison with the city and has witnessed triumph and fear; it has been a prison, a barracks, an imperial tomb and a sumptuous papal residence; it has seen munitions heaped up at the angel's feet and fireworks displays prepared on the occasion of joyous popular fea-

29.30 - **The Christian catacombs** originated in the 2nd century A.D. and continued until the 5th. From simple underground cemeteries, towards the end of the persecutions they became true sanctuaries of the martyrs and places of pilgrimage. Since Roman law prohibited burial within the walls, the catacombs developed along the major consular highways. There are more than 60 in Rome. Hundreds of kilometres of galleries with thousands of tombs (locules) excavated in the tufa faces, some containing the bodies of two or even more persons. Often with the symbols of the new faith cut into the tombstones. The photographs show the catacombs of Priscilla and St. Sebastian.

31 - **Mausoleum of St. Constance**. Built by Constantine as burial place for his daughters Constance and Helen, it was later used as a baptistery and became a church in 1254. It is the oldest cult building on a circular plan (c. 320 A.D.) and bears magnificent witness to the spatial sensitivity of the early centuries of the Christian era. The vault of the annular gallery is lined with splendid 4th century mosaics, some of the most ancient preserved in Rome, that reflect the style and motives of the mosaic art of the late Empire. The famous scene of the Putti harvesting grapes (a motive laden with allegorical/religious significance), made people in the 7th century believe St. Constance to be a temple of Bacchus.

32 - The story of **Santa Maria in Cosmedin** began in the 6th century and continued with enlargements and restructurings until the 12th, when it assumed its present form. The church contains art treasures of many epochs and is graced by a tall Romanesque tower, among the most interesting in Italy. The large circular stone preserved in its porch, known as "Mouth of Truth" (see No.16), gave its name to the square in front of the church, one of the most picturesque in Rome, on the site of the former Forum Boario. The space is enlivened by Bizzacheri's fine fountain with its reefs and tritons, commissioned by Pope Clement XI in 1715.

33 - **S. Sabina**, the "gem of the Aventine", as it has been called on account of the purity of its forms, possibly represents Rome's most perfect example of an early Christian basilica. Founded in the 5th century by Peter, an Illyrian priest, it was later – in 1222 – entrusted to the Dominican Order by Honorius III. At that time it became enriched by a bell tower, now demolished, and a graceful cloister. The interior is harmoniously paced by Corinthian columns of pure Parian marble. A precious jewel graces its atrium: the ancient wooden doors that go back as far as the 5th century, inlaid in low relief with scenes from the Old and New Testament.

34 - It would seem that the basilica of **S. Maria in Trastevere** was the first to be officially dedicated to the Christian religion. According to tradition, it was founded by St. Callixtus in 227 and completed by St. Julius in 352 A.D. The present structure goes back to the reconstruction of 1143, with subsequent addition of the bell tower, the ceiling and the chapels, eventually to be completed in 1702 by Carlo Fontana's portico. The many restorations that followed each other until the days of Pius IX did not change its appearance. The octagonal fountain, seemingly the oldest in Rome, was moved and restructured several times until 1692; it is the focal centre of this ever animated square, true heart of the quarter.

35 - **S. Clemente** is a typical example of the stratification of the centuries and cultures characteristic of Rome: two superposed churches of different epochs rest on similarly stratified Roman buildings. The early Christian church, discovered in 1861, dates to the 4th century and was dedicated to Pope Clement (88-97 A.D.). Destroyed during the Norman invasion in 1108, Paschal II rebuilt the upper basilica on the ruins. Outstanding are the Schola Cantorum, the fine cosmatesque pavement and the grandiose 12th century apse mosaic with the Triumph of the Cross. The Roman level comprises a Temple of Mitra (2nd/3rd century), a male divinity imported from Persia that found fertile soil in imperial Rome.

36 - **View of the city centre**. A composite panorama of the city's ancient heart, vividly rendered against the background of the Alban Hills by the early morning light. Cupolas, towers and altars enliven an urban tissue among the richest in the world as far as history and art treasures are concerned. The dazzling mass of the Victor Emmanuel Memorial dominates on the left, with the cupola of the Church of Jesus in front. On the right, the counterpoint of the cupolas of S. Agnese in Agone and S. Salvatore in Lauro. At the centre, from the rear, the tower of Palazzo Senatorio on the Capitol, the lantern of S. Ivo alla Sapienza, the small bell tower of S. Maria dell'Anima, and the low cupola of S. Maria della Pace.

37.38 - **S. Paul Outside the Walls**. Erected by Constantine on the base of Trajan's Basilica Ulpia, it remained Christianity's largest temple until the construction of the present basilica of St. Peter. The centuries saw it become a centre of spirituality and also the core of a fortified citadel. The building was almost completely destroyed by a great fire in 1823, and was rebuilt without sparing means. Surviving parts of the earlier church include the fine 13th century cloister with its gleaming mosaics, Vassaletto's paschal candelabra, the grandiose baldachin by Arnolfo di Cambio and some mosaics in the apse and the transept.

39 - **Santa Maria Maggiore** was erected by Sixtus III around 435 A.D., after the Council of Ephesus had proclaimed the Madonna "Mother of God". The building underwent numerous restructurings in the course of time, and elements dating to different periods have created a combination not devoid of intrinsic equilibrium. In the scenographic facade, for example, the 12th century mosaics could well prove less effective if they were not framed by the fine 18th century loggia. The massive Romanesque bell tower is the tallest in Rome. For many Romans this is the city's most beautiful church (for the interior, see Photograph No.41).

40 - **Michelangelo's Moses** in the Basilica of S. Pietro in Vincoli. The church derives its name from the chains that had imprisoned the Apostle, found in Jerusalem and custodied here. "Not only Moses", says a poster at the entrance to the church that illustrates the other important works preserved in the building. But today's visitor will come to this church mainly to admire Michelangelo's Moses, probably the world's most famous statue. The artist shows us the seated figure of the Prophet, proud and powerful in his solemn pose, the while he menacingly observes the idolatrous Hebrews. The statue was intended for the mausoleum of Julius II, designed for the new Vatican basilica, but unfortunately never completed.

41 - **Santa Maria Maggiore** (see also No.39). In spite of the many reorganizations and restorations undergone in the course of the centuries, the basilica still preserves its original character of an early Christian church. The interior sparkles with mosaics of different epochs that terminate with the splendid apse composition by Jacopo Torriti (1295 A.D.) representing the Triumph of Mary, one of Rome's finest mosaic masterpieces. The magnificence of the nave is further enhanced by the fine coffered ceiling designed by Giuliano Sangallo for Alexander VI in the fifteenth century and, as tradition would have it, gilded with the first gold come to Europe from the New World.

42 - The importance of **Saint John in Lateran** exceeded that of all the other patriarchal basilicas in Rome until the reconstruction of St. Peter's. Indeed, ever since the days of Constantine, the Lateran palaces had been the official residence of the Bishop of Rome and the church, erected in the 4th century, was called the "Mother of all churches". Following many vicissitudes, including wars, earthquakes and fires, St. John was repeatedly reconstructed, the last time in 1650, when Pope Innocent X entrusted the work to F. Borromini. The facade with its fifteen cyclopic statues was built in 1735. The church's many art treasures include the cosmatesque pavement, the tabernacle and the 13th century cloister.

43 - **View from the Janiculum**. The sunset twilight sets the city profile aflame in a limpid atmosphere that permits the gaze to arrive as far as the first peaks of the Apennine. The white mass of the Victor Emmanuel Memorial towers above it all, with its majestic quadrigas standing out against the snowy mountains and the fiery tiles of the Militia Tower that frame the king's colossal equestrian statue. By its side, the Aracoeli facade on the Capitol with the cupola of S. Maria in Campitelli in front. In the background, against the intense blue of the hills, the twin cupolas and the Romanesque bell tower (the tallest in Rome) of S. Maria Maggiore on the Esquiline.

44.45.46 - **Saint Peter in Vatican**. The old basilica, desired in its day by Constantine and completely pulled down in the 16th century to make room for the new temple, rose on the site where tradition placed the Apostle's tomb. The first designs for the new St. Peter's date back to the days of Julius II and Leo XI and were entrusted to Bramante, then Raffaello, Sangallo, Peruzzi and eventually Michelangelo, who realized the greater part of the body of the Greek cross and the cupola, while Maderno transformed it into a Latin cross in the first decade of the seventeenth century and constructed the facade.

The temple is of gigantic size, as can readily be seen by comparing it with the measurements of the largest churches in the world set out on the pavement of the central nave. It houses innumerable art treasures: one need only think of Michelangelo's Piety, the bronze statue of the Apostle attributed to Arnolfo di Cambio, the works of Bernini, like the pulpit and the baldachin with its spiral columns, imposing and scenographic emblem of reaching upwards for the Divine Presence.

What renders the Vatican complex such a unique creation is the ingenious layout of the square in front of the church, designed by Bernini around 1657. The immense colonnaded ellipse, connected to the church by two converging arms, harmoniously merges the basilica with a number of pre-existing elements, among them the Egyptian obelisk, the New Palace, the steps and Maderno's fountain.

47 - **Vatican Library. Sixtine Hall**. When Nicholas V decided in the 15th century to set up a public library, it had little more than 340 volumes. Sixtus IV brought the number up to 3650 and in 1475 officially instituted the library, providing appropriate accommodation. As the donations increased, Sixtus V had to build the quarters still used today, which were designed by D. Fontana in 1587 and have the Sixtine Hall as their outstanding feature. It is divided into two cross-vaulted aisles and is wholly decorated with grotesques and allegorical frescoes Today the library is one of the largest in the world, possessing more 70,000 codexes, 7000 incunabula, a million printed books and thousands of incisions and geographical maps.

48 - **Michelangelo's *Piety***. Sculptured at 25 years of age, it is the only work actually signed by the artist. Made between 1497 and 1499 for the ambassador of Charles VIII to Alexander VI, it is now preserved in St. Peter's. The Mother's foreknowledge of the Son's destiny is here expressed by Mary's youthful aspect. One is struck by the formal perfection, the compositional harmony and, above all, the intense pathos of this masterpiece that conferred fame upon its author notwithstanding his young age.

49.50.51 - **Sixtine Chapel. Michelangelo's frescoes.** In 1475 Sixtus IV commenced the construction of a "cappella magna" for solemn ceremonies. The very simple structure was probably conceived to render possible a grandiose decoration, free of constraints. Michelangelo frescoed the vault under Julius II, between 1508 and 1512. Sculptor by vocation, he transferred into a plane the three-dimensional solidity more in keeping with his genius. Four years of feverish work saw him, populate a surface of about 800 square metres with hundreds of figures. Principal themes of the work are the story of the Creation (No.51- Creation of Adam) and the original sin, Noah's sacrifice, the Great Flood and Noah's drunkenness, which occupy the central panels. All around there are the gigantic figures of Prophets and Sybils assisted by putti. The painted architectural structure gathers and orders the entire decoration into a perfect synthesis of architectural, plastic and pictorial elements, reflecting the unity of thought that characterizes the conception of the work

24 years later, commissioned by Clement VII, the artist returned to paint the Universal Judgement (No.49) on the front wall, completing it in 1541. The work implied the destruction of previous frescoes by Perugino and Michelangelo himself.

The impressive representation of the Day of Wrath reflects the ideological and religious travail of the Counter-Reformation The dramatic nature of the scenes, the violence of the demons, the terrible gesture of Christ the Judge, everything evokes an inflexible and severe law, an admonition to remain faithful to the Church of Rome. The immense scenario is sustained by a rigorous compositional balance that orders its reading. Everything revolves around the dominating figure of Christ, surrounded by the Virgin, the saints and the patriarchs. To his right the just are raised to heaven, sustained by angels, while on his left the damned precipitate, dragged down by demons. Hosts of angels in the lunettes sustain the symbols of the Passion, while a third group, lower down, sounds the trumpets of the Judgement. At the feet of Jesus, St. Bartholomew holds his own skin and there we discover the face of Michelangelo. In the 16th century, on the order of Pius IV, the nudes – considered scandalous – were partially covered by Daniele da Volterra, who was thereafter nicknamed the "pants-maker"

GENESIS
1 Creation of the light
2 God creates sun and moon
3 Separation of Waters
4 Creation of Adam
5 Creation of Eve
6 Original Sin
7 Sacrifice of Noah
8 The Deluge
9 Drunkenness of Noah
PROPHETS
14 Jonah
15 Jeremiah

18 Daniel
19 Ezekiel
22 Isaiah
23 Joel
25 Zechariah
SIBYLS
16 Libyan Sibyl
17 Persian Sibyl
20 Cumaean Sibyl
21 Erythrean Sibyl
24 Delphic Sibyl
Old TESTAMENT
10 Torment of Haman

11 Moses and the Brazen
   Serpent
12 David and Goliath
13 Judith and Holofernes
ANCESTORS OF CHRIST
26 Solomon with his mother
27 Parents of Jesse
28 Rehoboam with Mother
29 Asa with Parents
30 Uzziah with Parents
31 Hezekiah with Parents
32 Zerubbabel with Parents
33 Josiah with Parents

52 - **Sunset on the Tiber**. A splendid view - embracing St. Peter's, Hadrian's Tomb and the scenographic parade of Baroque angels on the bridge leading up to it - can be enjoyed from Ponte Umberto. From this distance one can appreciate the full grandeur of Michelangelo's cupola, which rises well above the body of the basilica. From nearby, in St. Peter's Square, the view of the cupola is disturbed by the tall facade later erected by Maderno. Unfortunately, the transformation of the building plan from Michelangelo's Greek cross to a Latin cross, and the forward shift of the facade stemming therefrom, have altered the relationship the cupola bears to the rest and the way it is visually perceived,

53.54 - **Vatican Gardens**. Inside the Leonine City there extend the carefully tended Vatican Gardens, rich in fountains, displays, grottoes and preciously decorated buildings. Noteworthy among the latter is the **Pius V Pavilion**, an extremely elegant building put up in 1561 by Pirro Ligorio for Paul IV, who desired a place immersed in green where could rest. Today the building houses the Pontifical Academy of Sciences. The delicious **Galley Fountain** is to be found in an out of the way corner of the gardens, at the foot of the Belvedere Tower. The highly ornate bronze model, which lovingly and in considerable detail reproduces a 17th century Spanish galley, was placed there in 1620 on a fountain dating back to the days of Paul V.

55 - **The School of Athens**. Struck by the talent of Raffaello, Julius II entrusted him in 1508 with the decoration of four rooms in the papal apartment, which the young artist transformed into one of the greatest masterpieces of Italian art. In the Room of the Signature the Dispute of the Sacrament represents the triumph of religious truth, while the opposite wall bears the grandiose School of Athens with Plato and Aristotle who debate about philosophic truth surrounded by their disciples and other illustrious philosophers of antiquity. The counterposition of the two frescoes expresses the humanist thought of the harmony of classical and Christian culture in search of the one truth.

56.57.58 - **The Pantheon**, dedicated to all the planetary divinities, was put up by Marcus Vipsanius Agrippa in 27 B.C. and completely rebuilt by Hadrian in 125 A.D. It is often considered the most significant monument of Roman architecture and is certainly the best preserved. Its great cylindrical body is covered by a colossal cupola, the largest ever constructed in masonry, with a nine-metre-diameter window at the centre, the only source of light for the entire temple. The diameter and the internal height are the same, 43.3 m. The entrance is preceded by a wide pronaos with 16 monolithic columns and crowned by a large triangular fronton originally decorated with bronze reliefs.

It was the first Roman temple to be transformed into a church (609 A.D.) and was named Santa Maria dei Martiri, which assured its integrity and maintenance by the popes. But the Christian images that filled the niches with scenes of the Nativity and the Annunciation appear like intruders in this spherical space conceived for the rhythms of pagan divinities. Much later the building became the mausoleum of the Kings of Italy and the painter Raffaello is also buried there.

The square in front of the "Rotonda" is graced by a fine fountain due to Giacomo Della Porta (1578) surmounted by an Egyptian obelisk. It has always been full of life, once a market, now a favourite meeting place of Romans, and is animated by very busy open-air cafés.

59.60 – **Trevi Fountain**. Famous throughout the world, this is the largest and most spectacular of Rome's fountains. A masterpiece by N. Salvi (1732-51), it is one of the most inspired and scenographic examples of Roman Baroque. At the centre of the mighty reef a colossal statue of Ocean moves forward on a seashell carriage drawn by two marine horses (the unbridled and the placid) held by tritons. He is flanked by the statues of Abundance and Salubrity. The fountain is fed by the Virgin Water, brought to Rome by Agrippa in 19 B.C. Tradition has it that you should throw a coin into the fountain if you want to return to the city.

61 - **Palazzo Spada**. From Renaissance times onwards, Rome enriched itself with splendid mansions, expression of the dignity of Rome's noble dynasties, especially popes and cardinals. A superb example of these kingly homes is the luxurious residence of the Capodiferro family (1540), subsequently acquired by Cardinal Spada (1594-1661), who had it restored by Borromini. The elegant facade with its fine stucco reliefs (1556) hides some magnificently frescoed halls with decorated ceilings. The photo shows the Corridor of the Stuccoes, which opens onto a very ornate courtyard with portico. Today the building houses a precious art collection, most works dating to the 17th century.

62 - **The Rape of Proserpine**. Masterpiece of Gian Lorenzo Bernini, sculptured in 1622 and now kept, together with other works of the artist, at the Borghese Museum (see No.77). Cardinal Scipione Borghese, favourite nephew of Paul V and untiring patron of art, had the young Bernini produce several statues for him. One of the most interesting is the group showing Pluto about to rape Proserpine. While the powerful figure of the god of the netherworld recalls the ideal perfection of Michelangelo's nudes, the morbidity incarnated by Proserpine reveals rather the desire for a more realistic and sensual poetry that was to be characteristic of many of the works of the mature artist.

63 - **Palazzo Doria Pamphili** is one of Rome's largest and most lavish mansions. Founded in the 15th century, it was successively acquired by various Roman nobles, eventually coming into the hands of Camillo Pamphili, nephew of Innocent X, who further enlarged the Aldobrandi collection. Noteworthy features are the elegant facade on Via del Corso due to G. Valvassori (1734), the magnificent 16th century courtyard, and the interior galleries and rooms (the photo shows the Gallery of the Mirrors). The art collection comprises more than 400 paintings dated 15th to 18th century, including Velasquez' famous portrait of Pope Innocent X. There are also works by Titian, Lotto, Caravaggio, Guercino, Ludovido Carracci and Lorrain.

64 - **S. Carlo alle Quattro Fontane**. Commissioned by the Barefoot Trinitarians in 1634, this little church on the Quirinal was Francesco Borromini's first autonomous work. He returned to work on its facade in 1667, but it remained unfinished at his death. Romans have always called the church "San Carlino", but – rather than a diminutive – this is a sign of admiration and incredulity: indeed, it is quite incredible how this church, complete with all accessory spaces, is constructed in an area no greater than that of one of the pilasters of the cupola of St. Peter's. The photograph shows the interior of the ingenious oval cupola lit by hidden windows.

65 - Borromini's cupolas of **S. Ivo** and **S. Agnese in Agone** frame **St. Peter's** in the twilight of a colourful dusk. The vibrant inventions of the Baroque against the background of classical perfection. Works far removed from each other as regards style and conception are unified by compositional balance and overall harmony. As if the view wanted to say that beauty is timeless and does not use any particular language. Even though the cupola was completely reinvented by Borromini: new forms and ornamental elements and audacious constructional expedients turn his work into a miracle of technique and style.

66 - Vault of the church of **S. Ignazio di Loyola**. Perspective illusionism was one of the techniques preferred in Baroque Rome for creating the idea of depth and space. 17th century vaults and ceilings were lined with architectural compositions opening towards the heavens and divine glories, real cupolas were provided with fake Baroque clouds, while faked cupolas were painted where real ones could not be realized. A past master in work of this kind was the Jesuit Andrea Pozzo (1642-1709), author of a theoretical volume entitled Perspectiva pictorum et architectorum. His masterpiece, the grandiose fresco on the vault of S. Ignazio, exerted a long-standing influence on late Baroque churches throughout Europe.

67 - **Fontana del Tritone**. Piazza Barberini would be nothing other than an opening between a series of chaotically arranged buildings if it were not for the famous Triton Fountain. It is the fountain, and only the fountain, that attracts the eye, that confers perspective and meaning upon the surrounding space. It has often been called Rome's finest fountain and – realized in 1643 - is certainly Bernini's masterpiece as a sculptor. And this in spite of the fact that it is rather sober and essential for a Baroque creation. A horizontal sea shell and four dolphins sustain the strong figure of an oceanic musician, whose breath produces a melody that abysses of time and space separate from our poor, distracted ears.

68 - **Stairway of Trinità dei Monti**. From Piazza di Spagna there rises the long stairway that, alternating flights of steps and terraces, leads to France's 16th century church of Trinità dei Monti. The ensemble constitutes one of the most vivacious scenographies of 18th century Rome, particularly in May, when the steps are lined all the way with azaleas in full flower. It seems that the French, who financed the work, wanted to place an equestrian statue of Louis XIV at the summit of the stairway, but the refusal of the popes, who certainly did not wish to have the statue of a French monarch in their city, commenced a lengthy dispute. Though devoid of a statue, F. De Sanctis' project (1723) at long last gained the approval of both parties.

69 - **Decorated facade of Palazzo Ricci (16th century)**. The decorative wealth of aristocratic homes is often presaged already on the outside by facades bearing stucco reliefs, graffiti or frescoes, the latter often complex in composition, but today – unfortunately – rather faded. From the fronts of these mansions there proudly project, not without artistic pretensions, the patrician coats of arms of their owners. The sacred images, usually situated at a corner of the building, numbered two thousand in the 18th century: they ranged from simple niches to more complex structures with paintings and sculptures. Significant and sometimes picturesque elements that have always characterized the urban scene.

70 - **" Pulcin della Minerva "**. The Egyptian obelisk in front of the Church of S. Maria sopra Minerva was found nearby and, as the hieroglyphics tell us, was erected in honour of the sungod at Sais in the 6th century B.C. The idea of turning it into a monument of allegorical significance goes back to Urban VIII, but it was completed only in 1667 to a design by G.L. Bernini. As explained on the plinth, the animal represents the Mind sustaining Wisdom as it strains towards Heaven. But the people's characteristic irony nicknamed it "porcino", piglet, which has come down to us in the more polite form of "pulcino", little chick.

71 - In the maze of the old city centre, the **Vicolo della Volpe** frames the graceful bell tower of S. Maria dell'Anima. It is one of those picturesque corners of the Rome of former days that have remained practically unchanged.
Indeed, the photograph reproduces the scene of Roesler Franz' famous water colour dating to the end of the 19th century without any obvious differences. Unfortunately, not all the city's nooks painted by the artist have had the same good fortune. Another suggestive and more important view, dear to artists already in medieval times, that has remained almost unchanged is the Tiber around Tiberina Island (see Photograph No.19).

72 - **Santa Maria della Pace** has received the attention of illustrious hands, from Baccio Pontelli to Donato Bramante – to whom the cloister is due - and Pietro da Cortona, who finalized the interior, the facade and the little square in front of the church. The consecration to Our Lady of Peace (due to Sixtus IV in 1482) transcends its purely religious significance and assumed clearly political connotations at a moment that, in Italy, was particularly uncertain and gravid with sombre forebodings of war.

73.74 - **Piazza Navona** combines the vital charge peculiar to places of meeting and amusement with an extraordinary series of historical and monumental associations, beginning with its shape, which faithfully reproduces that of the arena of Domitian's Stadium (86 A.D.). In the Middle Ages, while marbles, arches and stands were being demolished by time and men, the place maintained a certain rhythm of life. Games, markets and processions, which in Renaissance times became feasts and tournaments.

Gregory XIII had two fountains placed there at the end of the 16th century, with a drinking trough at the centre. The final transformation came under Innocent X, who could call on such talents as Rainaldi, Bernini and Borromini. And hence Palazzo Pamphili, sumptuous home of the Pope's family. And immediately after (1651) there came Bernini's masterpiece, the Fountain of the Rivers (No.74), a rock theatre in which the Nile, the Ganges, the Danube and the River Plate assume vividly gesticulating human form. And then S. Agnese "in Agone", Borromini's magnificent church with its splendid concave facade and twin bell towers, erected on the site of a very ancient church dedicated to the young martyr. The festive assemblies resumed in a greatly nobilitated frame. Week ends saw the square flooded for general amusement; and luxuriant 18th century ceremonies supplemented the Bengala lights and the water melon sellers portrayed by Pinelli.

75.76 - **Piazza del Popolo**. Porta del Popolo, the former Flaminian Gate opened in the Aurelian Walls, constitutes a scenographic entry into the city for visitors coming from the north, who have to pass this majestic facade dating to 1565 (No.75). The interior face was redesigned by Bernini ninety years later when Queen Christina of Sweden, who had converted to Catholicism, came to Rome. Even before crossing the gate, one is struck by the solemn symmetry of the "twin" churches of S. Maria di Montesanto (1675) and S. Maria dei Miracoli (1679), placed at the point of convergence of the three road axes of Via del Corso, Via del Babuino and Via di Ripetta. On the opposite side of the square there is the Church of S. Maria del Popolo, founded in 1099, reconstructed and decorated by the best Roman artists in the 15th century. At the centre there rises the Egyptian obelisk of Ramses II, brought to Rome by Augustus and erected here by Sixtus V in 1589.

In the 19th century the square was given its present appearance by G. Valadier, who succeeded in harmoniously combining the pre-existing buildings with the new works. The vast space assumed an oval shape, enclosed between two large semi-circ-ular structures decorated with statues and fountains. Other neo-classical fountains with Egyptian lions were placed at the base of the obelisk. The square was also connected to the gardens on the Pincine Hill by means of a monumental system of ramps and terraces (No.76), creating a grandiose scenography enlivened by groups of sculptures, reliefs, trees and fountains.

77 - **Paolina Borghese**. The Casino Borghese, erected by Giovanni Vasanzio (1615) in the park of the villa bearing the same name, houses "the queen of the world's private collections" (see also No. 62). The museum contains the collections of Cardinal Scipione Borghese, nephew of Paul V and great art lover, further enlarged by Cardinal Marcantonio at the end of the 18th century. Apart from painted masterpieces of world fame, the museum conserves some superb sculptures by Bernini and Canova. The latter is the author of the famous statue that shows Paolina Borghese, sister of Napoleon Bonaparte, as Venus.

78 - Particularly lively and popular, **Piazza Campo** de' Fiori is one of Rome's most authentic sites. A noisy market in the morning, a football pitch for local youngsters in the afternoon, during the evenings of the summer season restaurant and café tables appear all round the square. Here there once stood Pompey's Theatre (55 B.C.), but later the area became a grazing ground. Being normally very crowded, the Popes affixed their proclamations here and the square was used to execute death sentences. Giordano Bruno, today commemorated by the sombre monument at the centre, was burnt here for heresy in 1600.

79 - Hidden away near **Via del Pellegrino**, there is this picturesque little square, where a family of cats enjoys absolute tranquility. The presence of cats is one of Rome's most lovable characteristics. You will find them everywhere in the maze of the old city centre, idling in the sun on the roof of a car or on some ancient capital, erring in dark alleyways or spying passers-by from behind some crack. But Rome also offers them an enviable privacy between the fallen blocks of the forums and the ever-present old ruins, where the cats are undisputed masters at night. And then, the cats are at their ease in this city, because their character is rather like that of the Romans: a little sly, a little lazy, lovers of a good siesta…

The author's thanks are due to Fahim Avaregan and
Emanuele Folliero for their precious suggestions.

Translation: Herbert Garrett

Photolith: Pluscolor-Graphicolor (Milano)
Printed by Litografica Editrice Saturnia (Trento)
in the month of January 2005

Picture credits:
Archivio Vaticano: Nos. 47. 49. 50. 51. 55
SalaGroup: Nos. 62. 63. 66
Pubbliaerfoto: No. 6
Giacomo Giannini: No. 15
Euroedit: No. 2

ISBN 88-86147-45-7

Books of photographs by Giancarlo Gasponi published by Euroedit:

ROME REVEALED

Introduction by Enzo Siciliano
Text by Livio Jannattoni

260 pages format 24x30 cm.
202 full-page colourphotographs
Printed and plasticized slip-case
Available in Italian, English, French and German

The squares, the monuments, the markets, the people. More than 200 photographs vividly bring out the life and poetry of that extraordinarily composite universe that is Rome.

ROME - Water and Stone

Introduction by Giorgio Montefoschi
Text by Luciano Zeppegno

192 pages format 24x30 cm.
127 full-page colourphotographs
Printed and plasticized slip-case
Available in Italian, English, French and German

Fountains of Rome. From the famous ones to those hidden in courtyards, cloisters and grottos. A sample of marvels that have no counterpart of their kind anywhere in the world.

ROME - A special journey

Text by Livio Jannattoni

160 pages format 32x33 cm.
162 full-page colourphotographs
Printed and plasticized slip-case
Available in Italian, English, French, German, Spanish

A suggestive itinerary through the testimonies of Christian faith and art. From the simplicity of the early churches to the magnificence of St. Peter's and the caprice of Baroque.

PORTRAIT OF ROME

Introduction by Alberto Bevilacqua
Text by Glauco Cartocci

144 pages format 24x30 cm.
100 full-page colourphotographs
Printed and plasticized slip-case
Available in Italian, English, French, German, Spanish

A great theatre that has no equal, the Eternal City offers the composite spectacle of its different periods. A canvas of great variety and unforgettable suggestiveness.

The Magic of Venice

Introduction by Carlo Sgorlon
Text by Tiziano Rizzo

144 pages format 24x30 cm.
98 full-page colourphotographs
Printed and plasticized slip-case
Available in Italian, English, French and German

An intense and delicate portrait, where the Most Serene assumes the appearance and the colours of a dream. The luxury of the palaces, the magic atmosphere of the lagoon.

CARNIVAL IN VENICE

Text by Carlo della Corte

112 pages format 24x30 cm.
58 full-page colourphotographs
Printed and plasticized cover
Four-language edition (It, Eng, Fr, D)

A joyful dive into the gleaming Venice of carnival time. And behind the masks there appear the city's famous places and its most secret corners. A different and original way of rediscovering the city by the lagoon.

TUSCANY
A Marvel of Man and Nature

Introduction by Giorgio Saviane
Text by Marcello Pacini

200 pages format 24x30 cm.
152 full-page colourphotographs
Printed and plasticized slip case
Available in Italian, English, French and German

The magnificent art cities, the medieval boroughs, the grace of the countryside that inspired the Renaissance artists.

SPLENDID FLORENCE

Introduction by Giorgio Saviane
Text by Marcello Pacini

144 pages format 24x30 cm.
97 full-page colourphotographs
Printed and plasticized slip-case
Available in Italian, English, French and German

History and Treasures of the art city par excellence, cradle of the Renaissance. A thrilling trip amid the urban tissue with the world's densest display of works of art.

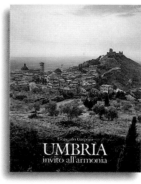

UMBRIA - Land of Harmony

Introduction by Pietro Lanzara
Text by Carlo Galimberti

216 pages format 24x30 cm.
197 full-page colourphotographs
Printed and plasticized slip-case
Available in Italian, English, French and German

A delightful voyage through Italy's green heart, where past and present still coexist in a wondrous equilibrium. The land of St. Francis and the captains at arms.

GLORIOUS CITIES

An elegant slip-case containing three books of photographs illustrating Venice, Florence and Rome.

Each volume has 144 pages format 24x30 cm with 98 colour photographs
Available in Italian, English, French, German

Introductions by: Giorgio Saviane, Carlo Sgorlon and Alberto Bevilacqua